THE little book OF DOGFULNESS

An Hachette UK Company
www.hachette.co.uk

First published in Great Britain in 2020 by Pyramid Books,
an imprint of Octopus Publishing Group Ltd
Carmelite House, 50 Victoria Embankment, London EC4Y 0DZ
www.octopusbooks.co.uk

ISBN 978-0-7537-3426-1

A CIP catalogue record for this book is available from the British
Library

Printed and bound in China

10 9 8 7 6 5 4 3 2 1

Publisher: Lucy Pessell
Designer: Hannah Coughlin
Editor: Sarah Kennedy
Editorial Assistant: Emily Martin
Production Controller: Lisa Pinnell

THE little book OF
DOGFULNESS

MINDFUL TEACHINGS
IN A DOG-EAT-DOG WORLD

"If you want to conquer the anxiety of life, live in the moment, live in the breath."

– Amit Ray

"If you
are mentally
somewhere
else, you miss
real life."

– Byron Katie

"The present moment
is filled with joy
and happiness.
If you are attentive,
you will see it."

– Thích Nhất Hạnh

"Allow yourself to rest. Your soul speaks to you in the quiet moments in between your thoughts."

– Anonymous

"Don't keep allowing the same things to upset you. Life's too short to live that way."

– Joel Osteen

"To see a world in a grain of sand and heaven in a wild flower, hold infinity in the palm of your hand and eternity in an hour."

– William Blake

"Life isn't as serious as the mind makes it out to be."

– Eckhart Tolle

"Thoughts are slow and deep and golden in the morning."

– John Steinbeck

"We spend precious hours fearing the inevitable. It would be wise to use that time adoring our families, cherishing our friends and living our lives."

– Maya Angelou

"When walking,
walk.
When eating,
eat."

– Zen proverb

"Learn to get in touch with the silence within yourself and know that everything in this life has a purpose."

– Elisabeth Kübler-Ross

"If you empty yourself of yesterday's sorrows, you will have much more room for today's joy."

– Jenni Young

"I don't have to chase extraordinary moments to find happiness. It's right in front of me if I'm paying attention and practicing gratitude."

– Brené Brown

"There are always flowers for those who want to see them."

– Henri Matisse

"Stop acting as if life is a rehearsal. Live this day as if it were your last. The past is over and gone. The future is not guaranteed."

– Wayne Dyer

"Compassion
is not complete
if it does not
include oneself."

– Allan Lokos

"There are only two ways to live your life. One is as though nothing is a miracle. The other is as though everything is a miracle."

– Albert Einstein

"Breathe.
Let go.
And remind
yourself that this
very moment is the
only one you know
you have for sure."

– Oprah Winfrey

"Today...spend more time with people who bring out the best in you, not the stress in you."

– Unknown

"In today's rush, we all think too much, seek too much, want too much and forget the joy of just Being."

– Eckhart Tolle

"We're all just walking each other home."

– Ram Dass

"Don't underestimate the value of doing nothing, of just going along, listening to all the things you can't hear, and not bothering."

– A.A. Milne

"Forever is composed of nows."

– Emily Dickinson

"Remember this...
that very little is
needed to make
a happy life."

– Marcus Aurelius

"Just as trees shed their leaves in winter and renew themselves, the mind can shed its prejudices, barriers and renew itself."

– Radha Burnier

"All of human unhappiness comes from one single thing: not knowing how to remain at rest in a room."

– Blaise Pascal

"Meditation practice isn't about trying to throw ourselves away and become something better, it's about befriending who we are."

– Pema Chödrön

"Write it on your heart that every day is the best day in the year."

– Ralph Waldo Emerson

"There's only one reason why you're not experiencing bliss at this present moment, and it's because you're thinking or focusing on what you don't have... But, right now you have everything you need to be in bliss."

– Anthony de Mello

"What lies behind you and what lies in front of you, pales in comparison to what lies inside of you."

– Ralph Waldo Emerson

"Be happy in
the moment,
that's enough.
Each moment
is all we need,
no more."

– Mother Teresa

"The most important decision you make is to be in a good mood."

– Voltaire

"There is nothing stronger in the world than gentleness."

– Han Suyin

"And now, this is the sweetest and most glorious day that ever my eyes did see."

– Donald Cargill

"You are the sky.
Everything else is
just the weather."

– Pema Chödrön

"Every day we should hear
at least one little song,
read one good poem, see
one exquisite picture, and,
if possible, speak a few
sensible words."

– Johann Wolfgang von Goethe

"Smile,
breathe,
and go
slowly."

– Thích Nhất Hạnh

"If you clean the
floor with love,
you have given
the world an
invisible painting."

– Osho

"You can't stop the waves, but you can learn to surf."

– Jon Kabat-Zinn

"Leave your front door and back door open. Let your thoughts come and go. Just don't serve them tea."

– Shunryū Suzuki

"Each day is an adventure in discovering the meaning of life."

– Jack Canfield

"Because of your smile, you make life more beautiful."

– Thích Nhất Hạnh

"Rejoice in the present;
all else is beyond thee."

– Michel de Montaigne

"Be the love
you seek.
Be the friend
you seek."

– Bryant McGill

"Today me will live
in the moment
unless it's unpleasant,
in which case me will
eat a cookie."

– Cookie Monster

"Somedays
you just have
to create your
own sunshine."

– Unknown

Picture Acknowledgements

Unsplash: Daniel Sandoval p.3, 63; Braydon Anderson p.4; Matthew Henry p.7, 19, 86; Delaney Dawson p.8; Emerson Peters p.11; Ekaterina Kobalnova p.12; Atanas Teodosiev p.14; Arjan Stalpers p.21; Charles Deluvio p.22, 28, 34; Tom Hills p.25; Tim Mossholder p.26; Richard Brutyo p.31; Brianna Santellan p.33; William Moreland p.37; Mike Burke p.38; Camylla Battani p.41; "Free To Use Sounds" p.42; Sophie Elvis p.45; Stephanie Cook p.47; Ja San Miguel p.48; Alvan Nee p.50, 79; Brooke Cagle p.53; Erda Estremera p.55, 65, 82; Ruby Schmank p.56, 77; Noah Austin p.58; Angelo Pantazis p.60; Daniel Sandoval p.63; Jorge Zapata p.66; Lacellia Pruitt p.69; Fredrik Ohlander p.71; Joe Caione p.73; Artem Sapegin Ugg p.74; Ruby Schmank p.77; Oscar Sutton p.80; Josephine Menge p.85; Kara Eads p.89; Gabriel Forsberg p.91; Alan King p.92; Jay Wennington p.94

Pexels: Pixaby p.17